To my amazing Mum, Sally, who always
found wonder in numbers. C.G.

To my little boys, Lucca and Vincente,
who make my world so BIG. G.K.

First published in Great Britain 2022 by Red Shed, part of Farshore

An imprint of HarperCollins*Publishers*
1 London Bridge Street,
London SE1 9GF
www.farshore.co.uk

HarperCollins*Publishers*
1st Floor, Watermarque Building, Ringsend Road
Dublin 4, Ireland

Text copyright © HarperCollins*Publishers* Limited 2022

Illustrations copyright © Guilherme Karsten 2022
Guilherme Karsten has asserted his moral rights.

ISBN 978 1 4052 9972 5
Printed in the UK by Pureprint a CarbonNeutral® company.
001

A CIP catalogue record for this title is available from the British Library.

Stay safe online. Any website addresses listed in this book are correct at the time of going
to print. However, Farshore is not responsible for content hosted by third parties. Please be
aware that online content can be subject to change and websites can contain content that is
unsuitable for children. We advise that all children are supervised when using the internet.

Farshore takes its responsibility to the planet and its inhabitants very seriously.
We aim to use papers from well-managed forests run by responsible suppliers.

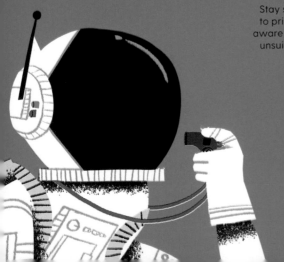

NUMBER SHOCKER

WRITTEN BY
CLIVE GIFFORD

ILLUSTRATED BY
GUILHERME KARSTEN

RED SHED

LATE ARRIVALS

If you squeezed all of Earth's history into 12 months, humans only turned up **36 MINUTES** before the end of the year.

The Earth started forming about **4.54 BILLION** years ago. A lot has happened since. If you shrank all those years into one calendar year, then the first life on Earth appeared in February or March. Plants didn't thrive on land until November. Dinosaurs turned up on the 13th December and died out **13** days later on Boxing Day morning.

The wheel was invented in Mesopotamia just 38 seconds ago.

The mighty Roman empire (established 14.2 seconds ago in 27BCE) only lasted for 3.5 seconds.

The last stone was added (c.2560BCE) to the Great Pyramid of Khufu in Egypt 31.8 seconds ago.

Compared to the lifetime of our planet, human history is all a bit of a rush. *Homo sapiens* have only been around for a tiny amount of time. On our calendar they did not turn up until **23:24** on New Year's Eve!

The first appearance (300,000 years ago) of *Homo sapiens* – people like us – was 36 minutes ago.

In China (c.1000ᴄᴇ), gunpowder was used to invent the first fireworks 7 seconds ago.

The United States (founded in 1776) has been around for less than 3 seconds.

Electricity in homes arrived under 1 second ago.

MOUTHY MICROBES

There's more bacteria in your mouth than on a toilet seat.

Every **6cm²** of a toilet seat may contain **1,000** bacteria. But that's nothing! Your mouth is home to as many as **6 BILLION** bacteria, made up of an amazing **700** different species.

Some bacteria do good by fighting germs and processing the food you eat.

Other bacteria help to cause tooth decay, gum problems or make your breath **PONG!**

Scientists estimate your body is home to about **39,000,000,000,000** (39 trillion) bacteria, fungi and virus cells. They outnumber your **30 TRILLION** human body cells!

Up to **2kg** of your weight isn't you – it's the microscopic creatures that live inside you!

!

E.coli bacteria found in your gut can double in number every 20 minutes.

ELECTRIFYING!

A single lightning bolt contains enough energy to make 83,000 slices of toast. Mmmmm!

The **5 BILLION** units of energy in a lightning strike can power

41,500

uses of a two-slice toaster.

Thunder is the sound you hear from the air heating up and expanding. It reaches your ears a number of seconds after you see a lightning flash because sound travels much more slowly than light.

Although lightning bolts can light up an entire sky, they are skinny – just **2–3cm** wide. The lightning heats up the air surrounding it, sometimes to a temperature of **30,000°C**. That's **5** times hotter than the surface of the Sun! SCORCHING!

Lake Maracaibo in Venezuela, South America, attracts more than its fair share of lightning strikes. Spectacular storms occur there about **260** nights each year and cause lightning to strike up to **15,000** times per night!

United States park ranger Roy C. Sullivan survived being struck by lightning SEVEN times!

WHAT A WASTE!

Over 1 MILLION plastic bottles are bought every minute, but fewer than one in ten bottles are recycled.

Many of the rest end up as rubbish in landfills or find their way into rivers that flow out into the sea. Swirling ocean currents help create giant garbage patches packed with plastics. The largest garbage patch floats in the Pacific Ocean over an area **3 TIMES** larger than France.

Some scientists estimate the Great Pacific Garbage Patch contains at least **1,800,000,000,000** pieces of plastic of all sizes.

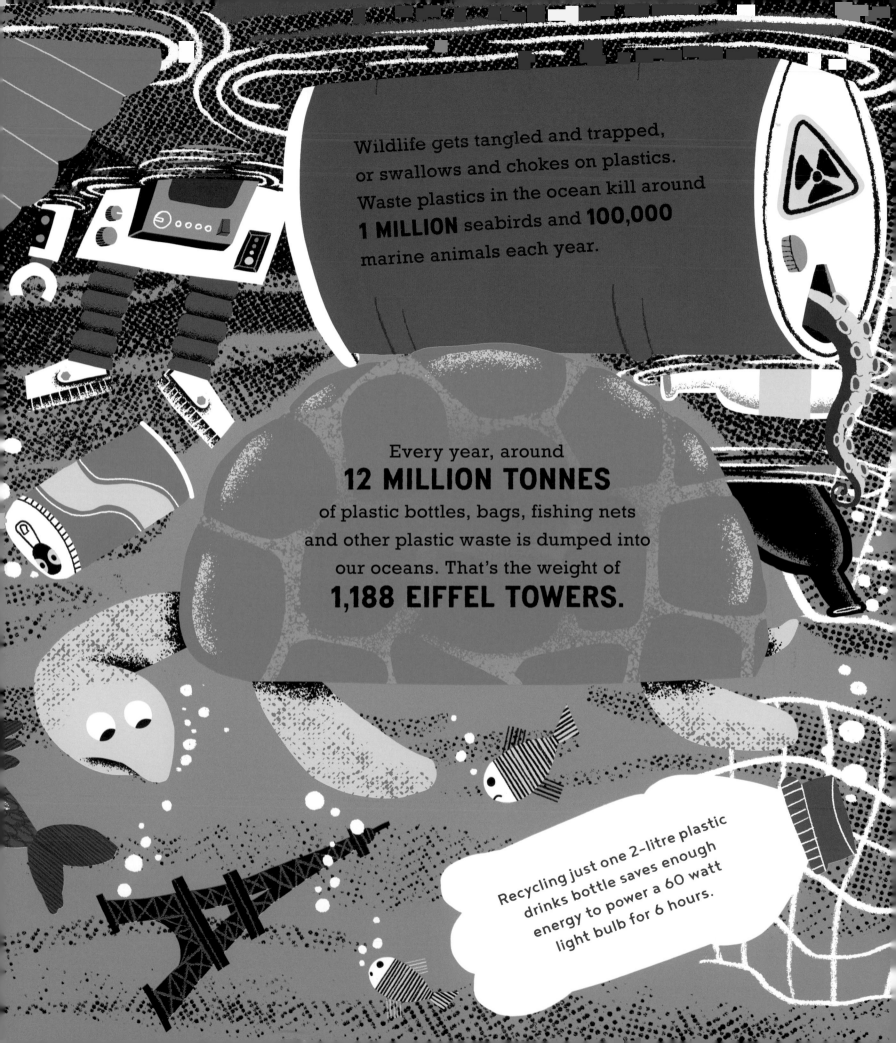

Wildlife gets tangled and trapped, or swallows and chokes on plastics. Waste plastics in the ocean kill around **1 MILLION** seabirds and **100,000** marine animals each year.

Every year, around **12 MILLION TONNES** of plastic bottles, bags, fishing nets and other plastic waste is dumped into our oceans. That's the weight of **1,188 EIFFEL TOWERS.**

Recycling just one 2-litre plastic drinks bottle saves enough energy to power a 60 watt light bulb for 6 hours.

ALL THAT GLITTERS

All the gold mined on Earth over thousands of years would fit into a **21m x 21m x 21m** room (that's shorter than a tennis court).

All that gold weighs around **197,600 TONNES**, about the same as **1,500 BLUE WHALES.**

There are more tonnes of cow's milk produced in the USA in a day than all the gold ever mined.

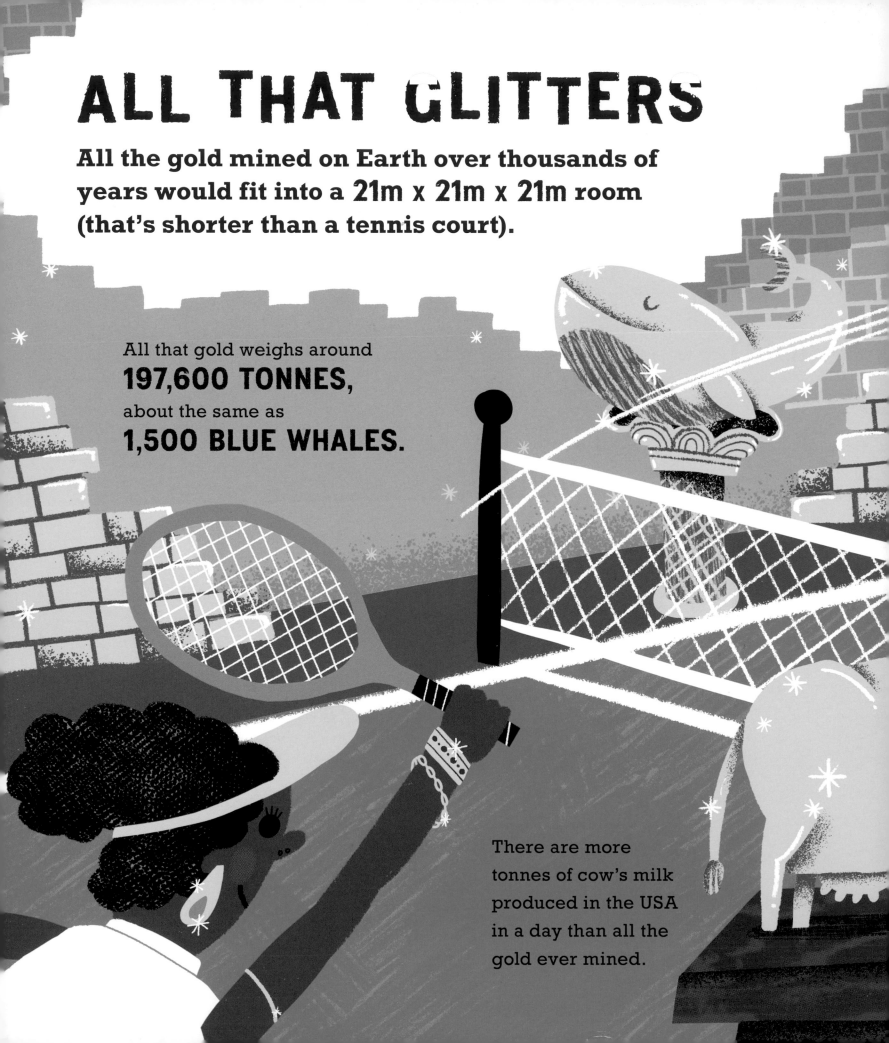

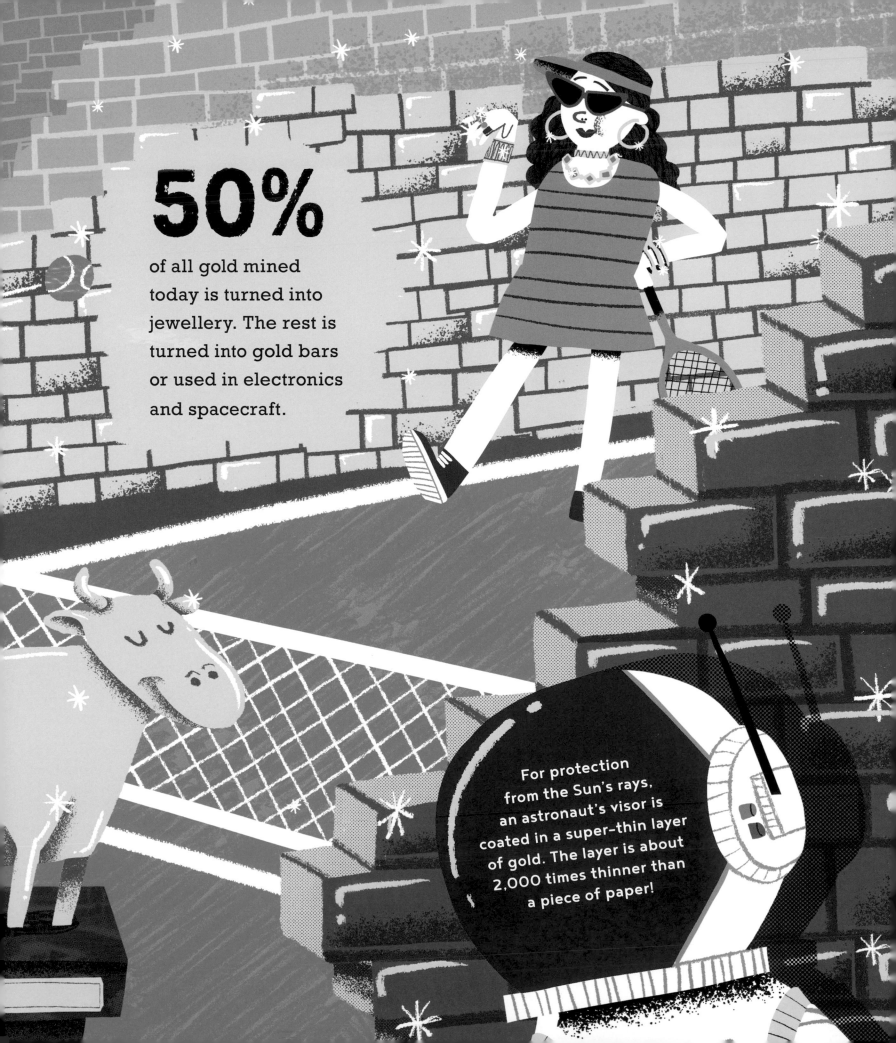

50% of all gold mined today is turned into jewellery. The rest is turned into gold bars or used in electronics and spacecraft.

For protection from the Sun's rays, an astronaut's visor is coated in a super-thin layer of gold. The layer is about 2,000 times thinner than a piece of paper!

BLOODSUCKERS

It would take 1.2 MILLION mosquitoes to suck all the blood out of a human body.

A typical adult person has **4.5–5.5 LITRES** of blood pumping round their body, and female mosquitoes tuck into the blood to help feed and grow their eggs.

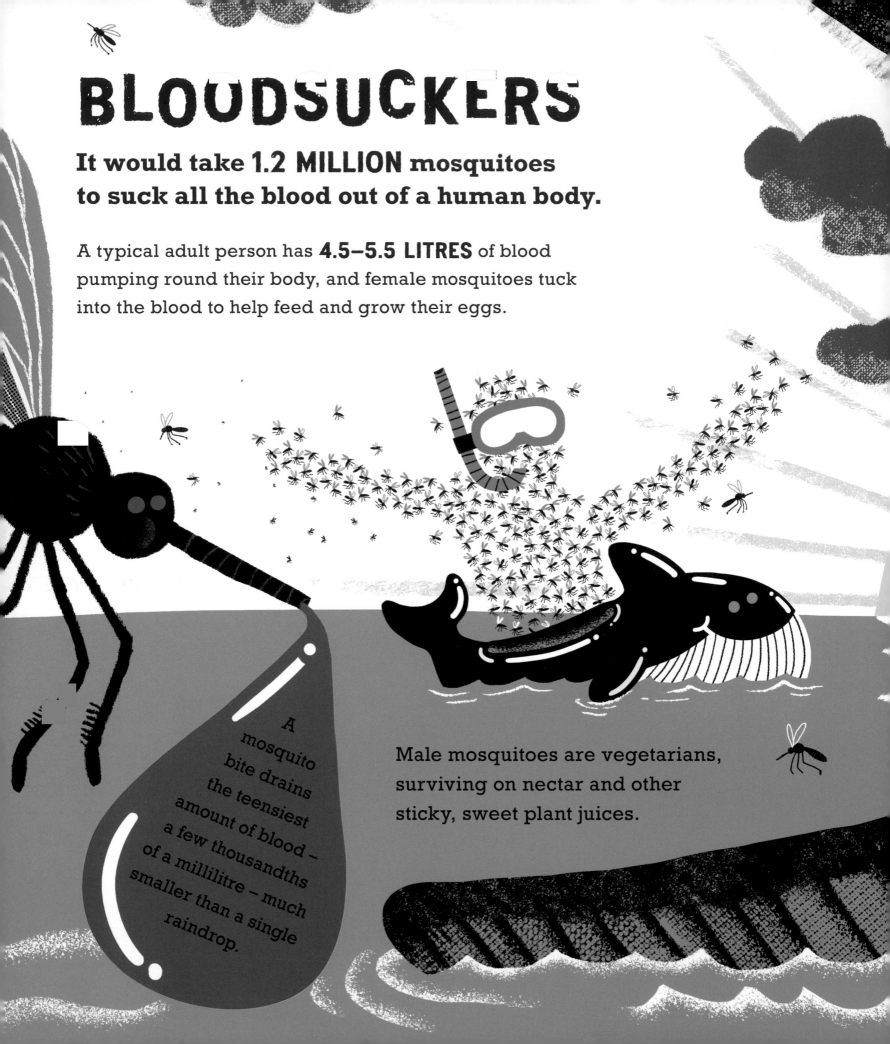

A mosquito bite drains the teensiest amount of blood – a few thousandths of a millilitre – much smaller than a single raindrop.

Male mosquitoes are vegetarians, surviving on nectar and other sticky, sweet plant juices.

Other creatures need **MASSIVE** meals every day to survive.

The whopping blue whale is the largest creature on Earth. An adult feasts on shrimp-like creatures called krill, which are the size of your little finger. But it scoffs an awful lot of them – up to **40 MILLION** a day.

An adult BLUE WHALE can eat up to 4 tonnes of krill a day. That's the weight of two medium-sized motor cars!

ELEMENTS OF SURPRISE

As many as **70** chemical elements make up a smartphone, but only **6** elements make up almost **99%** of the human body.

Elements such as iron, oxygen and carbon are the simplest possible substances, each made of only one type of atom. There are **92** of them and they act as building blocks to make everything – including this book and you!

You are mostly made up of these **6** elements . . .

CALCIUM
1.4%

OXYGEN
65%

NITROGEN
3%

CARBON
18%

HYDROGEN
10%

PHOSPHORUS
1.1%

A smartphone is made up of anywhere between **30** and **70** different chemical elements.

Silicon, oxygen, gallium and other elements form the microchips inside the phone.

Potassium and aluminium are often found in toughened screen glass.

A modern smartphone has

100,000

times more processing power than the computer on the Apollo spacecraft used to land astronauts on the Moon in 1969!

Nickel is used to help make the microphone.

The screen contains tiny amounts of rare elements such as indium and yttrium.

Wiring made of copper links all the electronics together.

Lithium and carbon are found in the phone's battery.

Tin and silver are used to help join wires and electronic parts together.

Neodymium makes magnets found in tiny motors that make your phone vibrate.

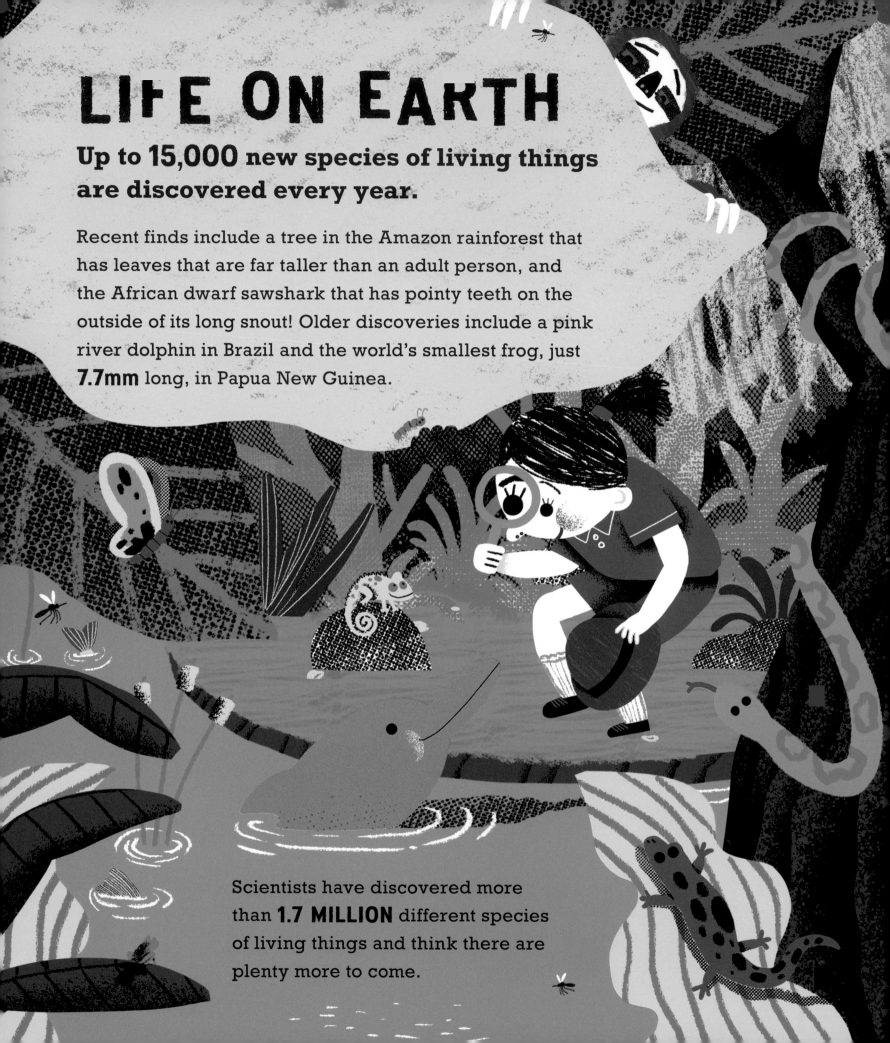

LIFE ON EARTH

Up to 15,000 new species of living things are discovered every year.

Recent finds include a tree in the Amazon rainforest that has leaves that are far taller than an adult person, and the African dwarf sawshark that has pointy teeth on the outside of its long snout! Older discoveries include a pink river dolphin in Brazil and the world's smallest frog, just **7.7mm** long, in Papua New Guinea.

Scientists have discovered more than **1.7 MILLION** different species of living things and think there are plenty more to come.

NORTHERN WHITE RHINOCEROS

SAINT HELENA OLIVE TREE

BERMUDA HAWK

CHINESE PADDLEFISH

At the same time, the sad news is that some living things have become extinct. They have died out, never to return. In the past 10 years, more than **160** species have become extinct. They include the animals and plants you can see in the cases on this page.

Scarily, a further **32,400** species including gorillas, the amur leopard, the bristlecone pine and **ONE-THIRD** of all frogs and other amphibians are in real danger of dying out.

The Laotian rock rat was thought to have died out 11 million years ago, but happily some were found alive and well in 1996!

PINTA GIANT TORTOISE

SPEEDY SPORTS

A badminton shuttlecock can travel at 426km/h – over 50km/h faster than the fastest ever Formula One (F1) car.

Mads Pieler Kolding from Denmark smashed the super-fast shot during a 2017 badminton match.

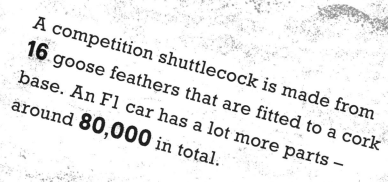

An F1 car can go from standing still to **100km/h** in just under two and a half seconds.

A competition shuttlecock is made from **16** goose feathers that are fitted to a cork base. An F1 car has a lot more parts – around **80,000** in total.

During a race, an F1 car's tyres heat up to reach **120°C** or higher – hot enough to cook an egg.

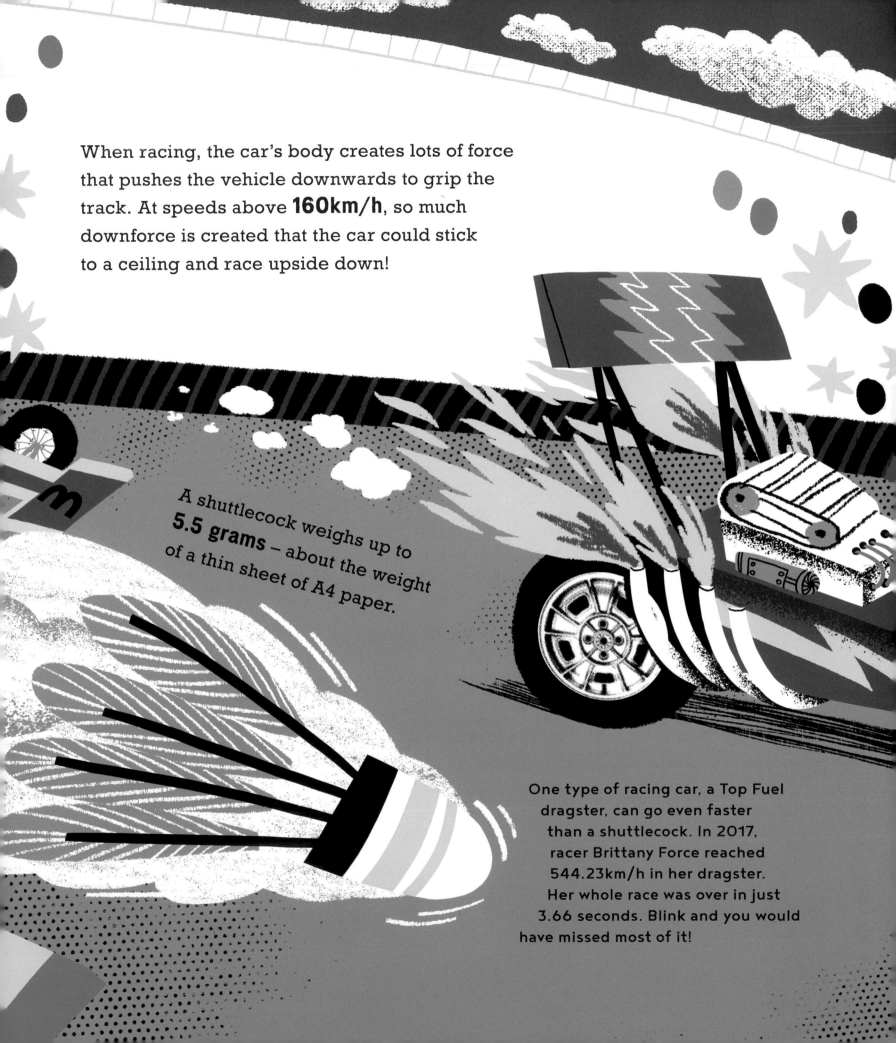

When racing, the car's body creates lots of force that pushes the vehicle downwards to grip the track. At speeds above **160km/h**, so much downforce is created that the car could stick to a ceiling and race upside down!

A shuttlecock weighs up to **5.5 grams** – about the weight of a thin sheet of A4 paper.

One type of racing car, a Top Fuel dragster, can go even faster than a shuttlecock. In 2017, racer Brittany Force reached 544.23km/h in her dragster. Her whole race was over in just 3.66 seconds. Blink and you would have missed most of it!

WOOD YOU BELIEVE IT?

We are losing a football pitch's worth of tropical rainforest every 6 SECONDS.

Tropical rainforests cover less than **3%** of Earth's surface yet are home to over **HALF** of all animal species. But the world's rainforests and the things that live there are under threat. Millions of trees disappear each year. They are cut down for their wood or to clear land for farming or new places for people to live.

These rich, wonderful, tree-packed places also house **TWO-THIRDS** of the world's plants, including many you eat and others used to make medicines to keep you healthy.

More than **10 MILLION KM²** of forests have been lost since 1900. That's an area bigger than the whole of the United States or **20 TIMES** bigger than Spain!

It's not just the forest that provides homes for living things – so do some of the animals that live there. Up to **900** different species of moths, beetles and insects, for example, can make their home in the fur of a sloooooow-moving three-toed sloth.

A sloth's top speed on the ground is about **0.21km/h**!

The world's largest flower is found in rainforests in Indonesia. Rafflesia arnoldii flowers can measure **105cm** wide and weigh **10kg** – about as much as two pet cats.

SHIPPING OUT

Around 90% of everything you buy is transported by ship.

You may never have sailed on a ship, but most of the things you buy and use have! Trade between countries depends on thousands of cargo ships criss-crossing the oceans. Most things are carried in boxes called containers.

A single container can hold:

12,000 shoeboxes

48,000 bananas

400 TVs

200 double-bed mattresses

60 fridges

At any one time, there are about **20 MILLION** containers on ships sailing across the oceans.

29,000 bath toys

MSC *Gülsün* is one of the world's biggest container ships.
Built in South Korea, it is **400m** long – the length of
8 Olympic swimming pools.

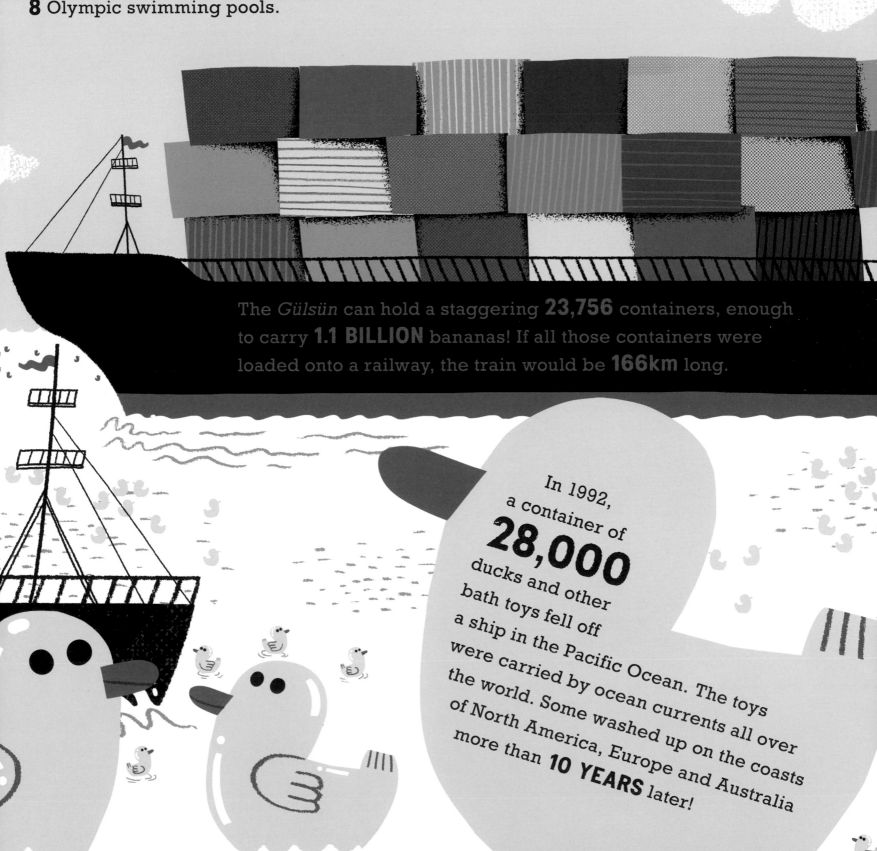

The *Gülsün* can hold a staggering **23,756** containers, enough
to carry **1.1 BILLION** bananas! If all those containers were
loaded onto a railway, the train would be **166km** long.

In 1992,
a container of
28,000
ducks and other
bath toys fell off
a ship in the Pacific Ocean. The toys
were carried by ocean currents all over
the world. Some washed up on the coasts
of North America, Europe and Australia
more than **10 YEARS** later!

MELTING AWAY

Antarctica is losing 7,191 tonnes of ice per second . . .

That's the same as **55** enormous blue whales or a giant herd of **1,200** African elephants. In a single day, **621 MILLION TONNES** of ice may disappear. That's more than the weight of everyone on Earth! Staggering, isn't it?

Where does it all go?

Rising temperatures mean the ice **MELTS** into the oceans.

The rate at which Antarctica's ice is melting is **6** times faster today than it was **30** years ago, and the Arctic ice around the North Pole is melting fast as well. Climate change warming up the planet has caused this.

Many scientists predict that by the year **2100**, seas could be **1m** higher than today because of all the extra water. This would lead to huge coastal floods and some islands and cities disappearing altogether.

IT IS NOT TOO LATE!

We can turn these shocking numbers around and slow down the rising sea levels. It is important to work together to tackle global warming.

DID YOU KNOW?

The Earth is spinning round at 1,670km/h — twice the speed of a jet airliner.

An Arctic tern can fly 1,200,000km during its lifetime — a distance further than flying to the Moon three times.

In 2020, Brazilian surfer Maya Gabeira surfed a world record-setting giant wave that measured 22.4m — as tall as a seven-storey building.

Every day there are around 22 billion toilet flushes. At least 141 billion litres of clean water are flushed down the toilet — enough water for half the world's population to each take a bath.

Over 25% of ocean species live in coral reefs, although the reefs cover less than 0.1% of the ocean. The Great Barrier Reef is home to at least 1,625 fish, 4,000 molluscs, and 133 shark and ray species.

In 2010, 1,760 PlayStation 3 games consoles were used to build a supercomputer for the US Department of Defense.

A typical adult man's bones weigh around 10.5kg — about the weight of two well-fed pet cats.

In one second 16,000,000 litres of water evaporate from Earth's surface — enough water to fill 6.4 Olympic-sized swimming pools.

The gold, silver and bronze medals used in the Tokyo Olympics contain metals recycled from 6,210,000 old mobile phones and other small electronic devices donated by the public.

100% of marine turtles, 59% of whales and 40% of seabirds have plastic pollution in their bodies.